Smoothies

Recipes of Smoothies for Health & Wellness

MARIA SOBININA

BRILLIANTkitchenideas.com

DEDICATION

This book is dedicated to my beautiful family and friends, as well as to you, my reader. I am happy to share the amazing joy of preparing healthy meals with you.

MARIA XOXO

Table of Contents

Introduction to Plant-Based Smoothies

One Ingredient Rule: Consume foods that consist of one ingredient in its natural, non-processed form, such as spinach, blueberries, carrots, beets, almonds, coconut.

Plant-based smoothies follow One Ingredient Rule. These smoothies are made of whole, raw, unprocessed, preferably organic, fruits and vegetables.

If you are on a budget and can't afford to purchase organic fruits and vegetables, you can use Environmental Working Group's (EWG) Shopper's Guide to Pesticides in Produce™ Rule of Dirty Dozen and Clean Fifteen.

EWG is a non-profit, non-partisan organization dedicated to protecting the health of people like you and me and the environment.

Dirty Dozen and Clean Fifteen Rule:

Dirty Dozen: strawberries, spinach, apples, nectarines, grapes, peaches, cherries, pears, tomatoes, celery, potatoes, sweet bell peppers, hot peppers.

Clean Fifteen: avocados, pineapples, cabbage, sweet peas, onions, asparagus, mangoes, kiwi, eggplant, grapefruit, cantaloupe, cauliflower, sweet potatoes, broccoli, cantaloupes.

It is preferable to purchase organic fruits and vegetables from the dirty dozen list. However, if you are to choose between highly processed foods and any item from the "dirty dozen" list, select the "dirty dozen" one-ingredient foods, even if they may contain more pesticides than the foods from the "clean fifteen" list. Whenever possible, however, purchase organic foods.

What is "Organic" produce? Department of Agriculture's National Organic Program certifies that food is grown without synthetic chemicals or fertilizers, genetic engineering, radiation, or sewage sludge.

Benefits of Plant-Based Smoothies

Plant-based smoothies are essentially raw foods. They offer the same benefits as raw foods:

-

- Reduce inflammation
- Improve and facilitate digestion
- Boost energy
- Clear up and make your skin glow
- Promote weight loss
- Prevent diseases, including cancer, Alzheimer's *and many others*
- Improve heart health
- Facilitate optimal liver function
- Provide more dietary fiber and prevent or treat constipation
- Provide essential nutrients for optimal functions of all body organs
- Anti-aging benefits
- Reverse hair loss and make your hair look shiny and beautiful

Health, Beauty, Longevity

When you consume organic fruit and vegetable smoothies every day, you will see a noticeable difference in your appearance, health, and vitality. You will have more energy, you will lose weight, and your skin will glow.

As time goes and you stay consistent with consuming plant-based smoothies, you may start looking younger, in some cases even one or more decades younger.

Everyone is different. Some of us consume more processed foods than others. Others eat whole foods and plant-based diets.

Depending on where you are coming from, the impact and results will be different. No matter where you are right now, you should expect to have positive changes in your appearance, health, and vitality.

Smoothies: Benefits of Detoxication

What is detoxification? Detoxification is a process of removing toxic substances from one's body. Our bodies are constantly undergoing the process of detoxification. The main organs that aid these processes are the liver, kidneys, lungs, skin and large intestine. Your body is working around the clock 24/7 to remove the toxins.

The word toxin is common. A toxin is any substance that can be poisonous to our body, including heavy metals, chemicals, pollutants, pesticides and more.

Toxins get into our bodies through the air we inhale, water, food, household, personal care products, prescription drugs, alcohol, and tobacco. Toxins are stored in cells, soft tissues, and muscles. Even your hair can store toxins.

Lately, our civilization has experienced an increased rate of cancer, Alzheimer's disease, obesity, diabetes, heart attacks, and autism in newborn infants. Many of these cases are attributed to environmental pollution and consumption of more complex foods containing chemicals, preservatives, artificial sweeteners, and artificial coloring to name a few.

Here are my top tips to help your body to eliminate existing toxins and to avoid adding new toxins.

- **Drink Plenty of Water**

You can either purchase water from a trusted brand or drink filtered water from a safe source.

- **Eliminate Artificial Sweeteners & Artificial Coloring**

While sugar is overall harmful to you, artificial sweeteners are ten times more poisonous than the former. Furthermore, artificial coloring is an outright poison consumption of which often leads to cancer. Eliminate both, artificial sweeteners and colorings from your diet.

- **Eliminate or Reduce Sugar**

Consider eliminating sugar from your diet. If you are not willing to eliminate sugar, reduce its intake. It is ok to have a piece of cake or an ice-cream occasionally. Many recent studies suggest a link between sugar consumption and diabetes, heart disease, mental health, and lately, cancer. For instance, Medical News Today published findings from a study revealing that a high percentage of mice fed a sucrose-rich diet developed breast cancer. There are numerous studies supporting similar findings.

- **Use the "One Ingredient Rule"**

One Ingredient Rule suggests consumption of foods comprised of one ingredient. These are whole foods in purest of all forms. For example, you may select orange, avocado, cashews, pork, chicken, coconut, to name a few.

The secret is that when you apply this rule, you are consuming unprocessed ingredients, and you limit the intake of additional toxins in the form of chemicals and artificial colorings. You should always try to get organic produce, whenever possible, as this further helps you to limit the intake of the toxins.

- **Consume More Fruits & Vegetables**

Raw organic fruits and vegetables are the best sources of nutrients. Even if you start consuming raw organic fruits and vegetables once a day, you will be making a leap towards a more beautiful, youthful and healthy version of you.

The easiest way to consume raw fruits and vegetable is to make a smoothie. For instance, you can replace your breakfast with a smoothie. A smoothie will give a good jump start into your day. Alternatively, you can replace your dinner with a smoothie. This will help you aid digestion, improve the quality of your sleep, and let your digestive organs to rest.

- **Select "Quick Exit" foods**

Some foods move faster through the body than others. Sometimes foods may stay as long as 72 hours or even more, while others pass through your body in just a few hours. Fatty meals, meat, and highly processed foods take longer to digest, and they take the longest time to move through the body.

The best quick exit foods are simple foods, like fresh, steamed or baked vegetables, fresh vegetable juices, avocado. Organic fish combined with fresh, steamed or baked vegetables and leafy greens is also a healthy selection.

When you consume green smoothies, your body receives essential nutrients. You also jump-start and accelerate the detoxification process.

Skin: Benefits of Detoxication

Your skin tone will improve, and it will become radiant. Your cells will be receiving vital power from fruits and vegetables. Raw fruits and vegetables have anti-aging properties to prevent and reverse aging.

Things to *Avoid* in Your Smoothies

Sugar: Use raw honey, banana puree, raw dates, or raw maple syrup instead of sugar.

Dairy products: If you would like to create a taste of a milkshake, add ½ cup of soaked raw cashew nuts and process in a food processor together with other smoothie's ingredients.

Artificial colors: Artificial colors are not good for you, and some are cancerogenic. If you want to add more brightness to your smoothie, add natural food colors, such as beet powder for red color, spirulina powder for green, turmeric powder for yellow, or blueberries for blue color.

Anything else: If you are using nuts, use them in moderation as they are high in calories, and it takes longer time to digest and pass nuts through your body. If you are replacing a meal with a smoothie add some nuts and you will feel fuller for a longer time.

Do Smoothies Promote Weight Loss?

Every day your body burns a certain amount of energy. To lose weight you need to consume a lower number of calories than your body burns. A common rule says: to lose one pound of fat it needs a deficit of 3500 calories.

Based on research and on my personal experience this number will vary from person to person. It will also depend on where you stand in your weight loss journey.

Furthermore, it will depend on the state of your hormonal balance. If your cortisol, thyroid, insulin, estrogen, and testosterone are in perfect balance, then the rule of 3500 calorie reduction per week to lose one pound of fat should apply to you.

If your hormones are out of balance, you may experience slower or faster weight loss. In my personal practice, when I was trying to lose weight, I observed that it may be quite difficult to jump start the weight loss process.

No matter how hard I would try, the weight scale number would not change. This could continue for a few months until my hormones become more balanced. At this point, the weight loss happened more rapidly and I was able to see the lower weight on the scale.

Having said that, just adding a smoothie to your diet, for most adults, will probably not lead to a significant weight loss. However, if you will consume a green smoothie on a consistent basis, you may experience balancing of your hormones, and it will be easier for you to lose weight by applying a common rule of 3500 calorie deficit per week to lose one pound of fat.

Smoothies as Meal Replacement

If you are trying to lose weight and use a smoothie as a meal replacement, you may see the weight loss progress. If you are consistent with drinking your smoothies, especially, green smoothies, once a day to replace one meal, this should lead to balancing your hormones, and later to easier and "less painful" weight loss process.

It is the best to either start your day with a smoothie, instead of your regular breakfast or have a smoothie instead of your dinner.

Having a smoothie for breakfast will power-start your day. You will feel more energized and light. This is especially helpful if consume heavy breakfast and highly processed foods. If you replace your breakfast with a fruit or vegetable smoothie you will see a big difference in the way you feel.

Alternatively, having a green smoothie instead of your dinner meal will help you have a better sleep at night, and to aid the digestive processes. A green smoothie will pass through your body rapidly letting your digestive organs rest at night.

You can experiment with what works best for you: a smoothie in the morning for breakfast, or smoothie in the late afternoon or evening to replace the dinner.

Fruits vs Vegetables, What's Better?

There is no simple answer to this. Raw, organic fruits and vegetables are the best source of essential nutrients, vitamins, minerals, and antioxidants. Raw, organic fruits and vegetables play a vital role in balancing your hormones. Various kinds of fruits and vegetables provide different nutrients.

Fruits contain more sugar. It is not the same kind of sugar as the white refined sugar you will find in donuts or pastries. It is raw fruit sugar that is unprocessed, and it is fully natural.

This type of sugar does not cause the same harmful effects as does the highly processed white sugar. However, you should bear in mind, because of high sugar content, fruits are quite high in calories. If your goal is weight loss, be mindful that fruits have more calories than vegetables.

Vegetables contain much less sugar and are more densely packed with the essential nutrients. These nutrients improve immunity, reduce inflammation, lessen the risk of type 2 diabetes, and reduce the risk of several types of cancers.

A good rule of thumb, 30% to 70% combination is good, where you will consume 30% of fruits and 70% of vegetables if you are trying to get more nutrients and lose more weight.

I, personally, love fruits. I consume a lot of fruits in smoothies, and I have no adverse effect on my weight. However, I immediately see an increase in my weight, if I start consuming highly processed foods. Be mindful of fruit sugars and chose the right combination of fruits and vegetables for you. Listen to your body.

Your body tells you what is best for you, by the way, it responds to the consumption of foods. If you feel light, vibrant and energized after consuming a meal, this food is great for you. If on another hand, you feel heavy, sluggish, and low on energy, it is time to stop consuming this type of food and eat foods that make you feel light, vibrant and full of energy.

In the next part of the book, you will find recipes for fruit and vegetable smoothies. Some of the smoothies contain nuts. If you are trying to lose weight, be mindful that nuts are high on calories. I hope you will enjoy the recipes and will have many positive effects on your appearance, health, and vitality.

Equipment for Making Smoothies

Blender *or Food Processor*

You will need a powerful blender to make a smoothie. Alternatively, you can use a food processor equipped with S-blade attachment.

Immersion Blenders

Stick Blenders

An immersion blender is a hand-held or a stick blender. These blenders are typically cordless, battery operated. You can use an immersion blender to blend a thinner smoothie, such as a fresh fruit smoothie. Representative brands are Cuisinart and Hamilton Beach.

Powerful Stick Blenders

-   These blenders are versatile kitchen appliances. Because they come with multiple attachments, they are multi-purpose kitchen appliances. Representative brands are Cuisinart and KitchenAid
-   Motor power 200 – 550 W
-   2 – 6 speeds, possibly with a turbo button
-   Measuring jar, blending jar, food chopper and

whisk attachments

Commercial Stick Blenders

- These blenders are more durable and can blend larger quantities of food. A representative brand is Waring.
- Motor power 200 – 750 W
- Longer shaft, more durable materials

Countertop Blenders

Jar Blenders

Jar blenders are stationary and usually placed on a countertop. They can perform varies kitchen tasks: blending smoothies, cocktails, mixing, pureeing, crushing ice, chopping, and more. Use this type of blender to make fresh fruits and vegetable smoothies. These blenders may have a tough time blending frozen fruits. Representative brands are Oster and Hamilton Beach.

- Motor power 100 – 300 W
- 0 – 2 speeds
- Jar capacity from 14 – 20 Oz

Smoothie Blenders

Smoothie benders, as the name suggest, are designed to make smoothies. It typically comes with a glass jar container which is dishwasher proof. Representative brands are Oster and KitchenAid.

- Motor power 200 – 1000 W
- Up to 7 speeds with pulse option
- Jar capacity from 58 – 72 Oz

Commercial Blenders

Commercial blenders are more powerful and durable and can blend a large variety of ingredients. These blenders can make smoothies from solidly frozen fruits and vegetables. Representative brands are Blendtec and Vitamix. I own a Blendtec, and I love it. Next time, I would consider a Vitamix blender because it has a tamper.

- Motor power 1000 – 1500+ W,
- to 7 speeds with pulse option
- Jar capacity from 58 – 72 Oz

Food Processors

If you own a food processor equipped with an S-blade, such as KitchenAid, you can use it to make a smoothie. Using a food processor is not an optimal way to make a smoothie, but if you do not plan to invest in a blender, a food processor will do a good job as well

Strawberry Banana Paradise

INGREDIENTS:

FOR THE SMOOTHIE:

2 **Bananas**, peeled

10 **Strawberries**, fresh or frozen

1 cup **Oats**, rolled

1 cup **Almond milk**

1 cup **Cashew nuts**, soaked *or 1 cup Plain yogurt*

2 teaspoons **Honey**, raw

1 teaspoon **Vanilla**, pure, extract

FOR THE ALMOND MILK: *(optional)*

1 cup **Almonds,** raw

2 cups **Coconut water**

EQUIPMENT:

High-speed blender, small mixing bowl, Serving glasses, measuring cups.

PREPARATION:

MAKE THE ALMOND MILK: *(optional)*

You can prepare almond milk at home, or you can also

purchase ready to use almond milk in a store.

Put one cup of almonds and two cups of coconut water into a blender. Blend it until it reaches milky consistency. Your almond milk is ready.

MAKE THE SMOOTHIE:

Step 1: Soak cashew nuts for 1-3 hours or overnight in a small mixing bowl. *(You can use plain yogurt instead of cashew nuts.)* Soaked cashews give your smoothie a milky taste without adding any milk products.

Step 2: Put all ingredients in a blender. Blend until you get a smoothie like consistency. Serve chilled.

To get the most benefits you should consume fruit and vegetable smoothies immediately. If you want to make the smoothie for later consumption, drink it the same day. Store in the fridge.

I am in Love

INGREDIENTS:

15 **Strawberries**, raw or frozen

1 cup **Cashew nuts**, soaked or 1 cup Plain yogurt

4 teaspoons **Cocoa powder**, raw, unsweetened

6 **Dates**, pitted

½ cup **Coconut water**

EQUIPMENT:

High-speed blender, small mixing bowl, Serving glasses, measuring cups.

PREPARATION:

Step 1: Soak cashew nuts for 1-3 hours or overnight in a small mixing bowl. (You can use plain yogurt instead of cashew nuts.) Soaked cashews give your smoothie a milky taste without adding any milk products.

Step 2: Put strawberries and dates into a blender and blend it until smooth. Pour 1/3 of the blended strawberries into a serving glass and set aside. This is the first "layer".

Step 3: Add soaked cashews to the blender with remaining strawberries and blend until smooth.

Pour ½ of the blended strawberries and cashew mixture into the serving glass. This is the second "layer".

Step 4: Add cocoa powder to the remaining mix in the blender and blend until smooth.

If needed, add some coconut water. Pour the mixture into the serving glass on top of the cashew layer. This will be your third chocolate "layer".

You will have a gorgeous three-layer smoothie. Serve chilled.

To get the most benefits you should consume fruit and vegetable smoothies immediately. If you want to make the smoothie for later consumption, drink it the same day. Store in the fridge.

Morning Glory

INGREDIENTS:

FOR THE SMOOTHIE:

3 **Bananas**, peeled

1 **Mango**, peeled, pitted

1 cup **Oats**, rolled

1 cup **Raisins**, golden

1 cup **Cashew nuts**, soaked or 1 cup Plain yogurt

6 **Dates,** pitted

1 cup **Almond milk**

2 teaspoons **Honey**, raw

FOR THE ALMOND MILK: *(optional)*

1 cup **Almonds**, raw

2 cups **Coconut water**

EQUIPMENT:

High-speed blender, small mixing bowl, Serving glasses, measuring cups.

PREPARATION:

MAKE THE ALMOND MILK: *(optional)*

You can prepare almond milk at home, or you can also purchase ready to use almond milk in a store.

Put one cup of almonds and two cups of coconut water into a blender. Blend it until it reaches milky consistency. Your almond milk is ready.

MAKE THE SMOOTHIE:

Step 1: Soak cashew nuts for 1-3 hours or overnight in a small mixing bowl. (You can use plain yogurt instead of cashew nuts.) Soaked cashews give your smoothie a milky taste without adding any milk products.

Step 2: Put all ingredients in a blender. Blend until you get a smoothie like consistency. Serve chilled.

To get the most benefits you should consume fruit and vegetable smoothies immediately. If you want to make the smoothie for later consumption, drink it the same day. Store in the fridge.

Going Nuts

INGREDIENTS:

FOR THE SMOOTHIE:

3 **Bananas**, peeled

1 cup **Raisins**, brown

1 cup **Apricots**, dried

1 cup **Cherries**, dried

1 cup **Cashew nuts**, soaked *or 1 cup Plain yogurt*

1 cup **Brazil**, nuts

6 **Dates**, pitted

1 cup **Almond Milk**

2 teaspoons **Honey**, raw

FOR THE ALMOND MILK: *(optional)*

1 cup **Almonds,** raw

2 cups **Coconut water**

EQUIPMENT:

High-speed blender, small mixing bowl, Serving glasses, measuring cups.

PREPARATION:

MAKE THE ALMOND MILK: *(optional)*

You can prepare almond milk at home, or you can also purchase ready to use almond milk in a store.

Put one cup of almonds and two cups of coconut water into a blender. Blend it until it reaches milky consistency. Your almond milk is ready.

MAKE THE SMOOTHIE:

Step 1: Soak cashew nuts for 1-3 hours or overnight in a small mixing bowl. *(You can use plain yogurt instead of cashew nuts.)* Soaked cashews give your smoothie a milky taste without adding any milk products.

Step 2: Put all ingredients in a blender. Blend until you get a smoothie like consistency. Serve chilled.

To get the most benefits you should consume fruit and vegetable smoothies immediately. If you want to make the smoothie for later consumption, drink it the same day. Store in the fridge.

Fruit Blend

INGREDIENTS:

FOR THE SMOOTHIE:

1 **Avocado**, peeled, pitted

1 **Mango**, peeled, pitted

1 cup **Apricots**, dried

1 cup **Pineapple**, dried

1 cup **Cashew nuts**, soaked *or 1 cup Plain yogurt*

1 cup **Brazil nuts**

6 **Dates**, pitted

2 cups **Almond Milk**

2 teaspoons **Honey**, raw

FOR THE ALMOND MILK: *(optional)*

1 cup **Almonds,** raw

2 cups **Coconut water**

EQUIPMENT:

High-speed blender, small mixing bowl, Serving glasses, measuring cups.

PREPARATION:

MAKE THE ALMOND MILK: *(optional)*

You can prepare almond milk at home, or you can also purchase ready to use almond milk in a store.

Put one cup of almonds and two cups of coconut water into a blender. Blend it until it reaches milky consistency. Your almond milk is ready.

MAKE THE SMOOTHIE:

Step 1: Soak cashew nuts for 1-3 hours or overnight in a small mixing bowl. *(You can use plain yogurt instead of cashew nuts.)* Soaked cashews give your smoothie a milky taste without adding any milk products.

Step 2: Put all ingredients in a blender. Blend until you get a smoothie like consistency. Serve chilled.

To get the most benefits you should consume fruit and vegetable smoothies immediately. If you want to make the smoothie for later consumption, drink it the same day. Store in the fridge.

Chocolate Sundays

INGREDIENTS:

FOR THE SMOOTHIE:

1 **Avocado**, peeled, pitted

1 **Mango**, peeled, pitted

1 cup **Cocoa powder,** raw, unprocessed

1 cup **Cashew nuts**, soaked *or 1 cup Plain yogurt*

6 **Dates**, pitted

2 cups **Almond Milk**

2 teaspoons **Honey**, raw

FOR THE ALMOND MILK: *(optional)*

1 cup **Almonds,** raw

2 cups **Coconut water**

EQUIPMENT:

High-speed blender, small mixing bowl, Serving glasses, measuring cups.

PREPARATION:

MAKE THE ALMOND MILK: *(optional)*

You can prepare almond milk at home, or you can also

purchase ready to use almond milk in a store.

Put one cup of almonds and two cups of coconut water into a blender. Blend it until it reaches milky consistency. Your almond milk is ready.

MAKE THE SMOOTHIE:

Step 1: Soak cashew nuts for 1-3 hours or overnight in a small mixing bowl. *(You can use plain yogurt instead of cashew nuts.)* Soaked cashews give your smoothie a milky taste without adding any milk products.

Step 2: Put all ingredients in a blender. Blend until you get a smoothie like consistency. Serve chilled.

To get the most benefits you should consume fruit and vegetable smoothies immediately. If you want to make the smoothie for later consumption, drink it the same day. Store in the fridge.

TGIF

INGREDIENTS:

FOR THE SMOOTHIE:

2 **Bananas**, peeled

1 cup **Raspberries,** fresh or frozen

1 cup **Cocoa powder,** raw, unprocessed

1 cup **Cashew nuts**, soaked *or 1 cup Plain yogurt*

6 **Dates**, pitted

2 cups **Almond Milk**

2 teaspoons **Honey**, raw

1 inch **Vanilla bean**

FOR THE ALMOND MILK: *(optional)*

1 cup **Almonds,** raw

2 cups **Coconut water**

EQUIPMENT:

High-speed blender, small mixing bowl, Serving glasses, measuring cups.

PREPARATION:

MAKE THE ALMOND MILK: *(optional)*

You can prepare almond milk at home, or you can also purchase ready to use almond milk in a store.

Put one cup of almonds and two cups of coconut water into a blender. Blend it until it reaches milky consistency. Your almond milk is ready.

MAKE THE SMOOTHIE:

Step 1: Soak cashew nuts for 1-3 hours or overnight in a small mixing bowl. *(You can use plain yogurt instead of cashew nuts.)* Soaked cashews give your smoothie a milky taste without adding any milk products.

Step 2: Put all ingredients in a blender. Blend until you get a smoothie like consistency. Serve chilled.

To get the most benefits you should consume fruit and vegetable smoothies immediately. If you want to make the smoothie for later consumption, drink it the same day. Store in the fridge.

For my Sweetheart

INGREDIENTS:

1 cup **Blueberries,** fresh or frozen

1 cup **Raspberries,** fresh or frozen

10 **Strawberries,** fresh or frozen

6 **Dates**, pitted

2 cups **Almond Milk**

2 teaspoons **Honey**, raw

1 inch **Vanilla bean**

FOR THE ALMOND MILK: *(optional)*

1 cup **Almonds,** raw

2 cups **Coconut water**

EQUIPMENT:

High-speed blender, small mixing bowl, Serving glasses, measuring cups.

PREPARATION:

MAKE THE ALMOND MILK: *(optional)*

You can prepare almond milk at home, or you can also purchase ready to use almond milk in a store.

Put one cup of almonds and two cups of coconut water into a blender. Blend it until it reaches milky consistency. Your almond milk is ready.

MAKE THE SMOOTHIE:

Step 1: Soak cashew nuts for 1-3 hours or overnight in a small mixing bowl. *(You can use plain yogurt instead of cashew nuts.)* Soaked cashews give your smoothie a milky taste without adding any milk products.

Step 2: Put all ingredients in a blender. Blend until you get a smoothie like consistency. Serve chilled.

To get the most benefits you should consume fruit and vegetable smoothies immediately. If you want to make the smoothie for later consumption, drink it the same day. Store in the fridge.

Yellow Sweets

INGREDIENTS:

1 **Banana**, peeled

1 **Grapefruit**, juice of

2 **Oranges**, juice of

6 **Dates**, pitted

1 inch **Vanilla bean**

EQUIPMENT:

High-speed blender, Serving glasses, measuring cups.

PREPARATION:

Put all ingredients in a blender. Blend until you get a smoothie like consistency. Serve chilled.

To get the most benefits you should consume fruit and vegetable smoothies immediately. If you want to make the smoothie for later consumption, drink it the same day. Store in the fridge.

Monday Morning

INGREDIENTS:

1 cup **Kale,** fresh

1 cup **Spinach,** fresh

1 **Grapefruit,** juice of

EQUIPMENT:

High-speed blender, Serving glasses, measuring cups.

PREPARATION:

Put all ingredients in a blender. Blend until you get a smoothie like consistency. Serve chilled.

To get the most benefits you should consume fruit and vegetable smoothies immediately. If you want to make the smoothie for later consumption, drink it the same day. Store in the fridge.

Going Green

INGREDIENTS:

1 **Cucumber**, fresh

2 **Celery stalks**, fresh

1 **Grapefruit**, juice of

1 cup **Spinach,** fresh

1 **Grapefruit,** juice of

EQUIPMENT:

High-speed blender, Serving glasses, measuring cups.

PREPARATION:

Put all ingredients in a blender. Blend until you get a smoothie like consistency. Serve chilled.

To get the most benefits you should consume fruit and vegetable smoothies immediately. If you want to make the smoothie for later consumption, drink it the same day. Store in the fridge.

Green Tea Raspberry

INGREDIENTS:

2 cups **Raspberries**

5 **Strawberries**

1 cup **Tea**, green

3 teaspoons **Cocoa powder**, raw, unsweetened

EQUIPMENT:

High-speed blender, Serving glasses, measuring cups.

PREPARATION:

Put all ingredients in a blender. Blend until you get a smoothie like consistency. Serve chilled.

To get the most benefits you should consume fruit and vegetable smoothies immediately. If you want to make the smoothie for later consumption, drink it the same day. Store in the fridge.

Tai Secrets

INGREDIENTS:

2 cups **Young coconut,** the meat of

½ **Pineapple**, fresh

1 **Mango**, peeled, pitted

3 teaspoons **Cocoa powder**, raw, unsweetened

EQUIPMENT:

High-speed blender, Serving glasses, measuring cups.

PREPARATION:

Put all ingredients in a blender. Blend until you get a smoothie like consistency. Serve chilled.

To get the most benefits you should consume fruit and vegetable smoothies immediately. If you want to make the smoothie for later consumption, drink it the same day. Store in the fridge.

Going Bananas

INGREDIENTS:

5 **Bananas**, peeled

4 teaspoons **Cocoa powder**, raw, unsweetened

½ cup **Coconut** water

EQUIPMENT:

High-speed blender, Serving glasses, measuring cups.

PREPARATION:

Put all ingredients in a blender. Blend until you get a smoothie like consistency. Serve chilled.

To get the most benefits you should consume fruit and vegetable smoothies immediately. If you want to make the smoothie for later consumption, drink it the same day. Store in the fridge.

Blueberry Banana

INGREDIENTS:

FOR THE SMOOTHIE:

2 **Bananas**, peeled

2 cups **Blueberries,** fresh or frozen

1 cup Oats, rolled

1 cup Almond milk

1 cup **Cashew nuts**, soaked *or 1 cup Plain yogurt*

6 **Dates**, pitted

2 teaspoons **Honey**, raw

1 inch **Vanilla bean**

1 pinch **Cinnamon**, powder

FOR THE ALMOND MILK: *(optional)*

1 cup **Almonds,** raw

2 cups **Coconut water**

EQUIPMENT:

High-speed blender, small mixing bowl, Serving glasses, measuring cups.

PREPARATION:

MAKE THE ALMOND MILK: *(optional)*

You can prepare almond milk at home, or you can also purchase ready to use almond milk in a store.

Put one cup of almonds and two cups of coconut water into a blender. Blend it until it reaches milky consistency. Your almond milk is ready.

MAKE THE SMOOTHIE:

Step 1: Soak cashew nuts for 1-3 hours or overnight in a small mixing bowl. *(You can use plain yogurt instead of cashew nuts.)* Soaked cashews give your smoothie a milky taste without adding any milk products.

Step 2: Put all ingredients in a blender. Blend until you get a smoothie like consistency. Serve chilled.

To get the most benefits you should consume fruit and vegetable smoothies immediately. If you want to make the smoothie for later consumption, drink it the same day. Store in the fridge.

Banana Yogurt

INGREDIENTS:

5 **Bananas**, peeled

1 cup **Cashew nuts**, soaked *or 1 cup Plain yogurt*

6 **Dates**, pitted

½ cup **Coconut water**

EQUIPMENT:

High-speed blender, small mixing bowl, Serving glasses, measuring cups.

PREPARATION:

Step 1: Soak cashew nuts for 1-3 hours or overnight in a small mixing bowl. *(You can use plain yogurt instead of cashew nuts.)* Soaked cashews give your smoothie a milky taste without adding any milk products.

Step 2: Put all ingredients in a blender. Blend until you get a smoothie like consistency. Serve chilled.

To get the most benefits you should consume fruit and vegetable smoothies immediately. If you want to make the smoothie for later consumption, drink it the same day. Store in the fridge.

Mango Yogurt

INGREDIENTS:

3 **Mangos**, peeled, pitted

1 cup **Cashew nuts**, soaked *or 1 cup Plain yogurt*

6 **Dates**, pitted

½ cup **Coconut water**

EQUIPMENT:

High-speed blender, small mixing bowl, Serving glasses, measuring cups.

PREPARATION:

Step 1: Soak cashew nuts for 1-3 hours or overnight in a small mixing bowl. *(You can use plain yogurt instead of cashew nuts.)* Soaked cashews give your smoothie a milky taste without adding any milk products.

Step 2: Put all ingredients in a blender. Blend until you get a smoothie like consistency. Serve chilled.

To get the most benefits you should consume fruit and vegetable smoothies immediately. If you want to make the smoothie for later consumption, drink it the same day. Store in the fridge.

Green Glow

INGREDIENTS:

1 **Avocado**, peeled, pitted

2 **Cucumbers**, fresh

2 teaspoons **Wheatgrass**, powdered

1 cup **Tea**, green

EQUIPMENT:

High-speed blender, Serving glasses, measuring cups.

PREPARATION:

Put all ingredients in a blender. Blend until you get a smoothie like consistency. Serve chilled.

To get the most benefits you should consume fruit and vegetable smoothies immediately. If you want to make the smoothie for later consumption, drink it the same day. Store in the fridge.

Mellow Mellon

INGREDIENTS:

½ **Melon**, peeled, pitted

1 **Lime**, peeled, pitted

EQUIPMENT:

High-speed blender, Serving glasses, measuring cups.

PREPARATION:

Put all ingredients in a blender. Blend until you get a smoothie like consistency. Serve chilled.

To get the most benefits you should consume fruit and vegetable smoothies immediately. If you want to make the smoothie for later consumption, drink it the same day. Store in the fridge.

Light Start

INGREDIENTS:

½ **Watermelon**, peeled, pitted

1 **Lime**, peeled, pitted

EQUIPMENT:

High-speed blender, Serving glasses, measuring cups.

PREPARATION:

Put all ingredients in a blender. Blend until you get a smoothie like consistency. Serve chilled.

To get the most benefits you should consume fruit and vegetable smoothies immediately. If you want to make the smoothie for later consumption, drink it the same day. Store in the fridge.

South Beach

INGREDIENTS:

3 **Mangos**, peeled, pitted

1 **Orange**, juice of

1 cup **Young coconut,** the meat of

EQUIPMENT:

High-speed blender, Serving glasses, measuring cups.

PREPARATION:

Put all ingredients in a blender. Blend until you get a smoothie like consistency. Serve chilled.

To get the most benefits you should consume fruit and vegetable smoothies immediately. If you want to make the smoothie for later consumption, drink it the same day. Store in the fridge.

Starburst

INGREDIENTS:

1 cup **Blueberries**, fresh or frozen

1 cup **Raspberries**, fresh or frozen

1 cup **Strawberries**, fresh or frozen

1 cup **Cashew nuts**, soaked *or 1 cup Plain yogurt*

1 cup **Tea**, green

EQUIPMENT:

High-speed blender, small mixing bowl, Serving glasses, measuring cups.

PREPARATION:

Step 1: Soak cashew nuts for 1-3 hours or overnight in a small mixing bowl. *(You can use plain yogurt instead of cashew nuts.)* Soaked cashews give your smoothie a milky taste without adding any milk products.

Step 2: Put all ingredients in a blender. Blend until you get a smoothie like consistency. Serve chilled.

To get the most benefits you should consume fruit and vegetable smoothies immediately. If you want to make the smoothie for later consumption, drink it the same day. Store in the fridge.

Pineapple Yogurt

INGREDIENTS:

½ **Pineapple**, fresh, peeled

1 cup **Cashew nuts**, soaked *or 1 cup Plain yogurt*

6 **Dates**, pitted

½ cup **Coconut water**

EQUIPMENT:

High-speed blender, small mixing bowl, Serving glasses, measuring cups.

PREPARATION:

Step 1: Soak cashew nuts for 1-3 hours or overnight in a small mixing bowl. *(You can use plain yogurt instead of cashew nuts.)* Soaked cashews give your smoothie a milky taste without adding any milk products.

Step 2: Put all ingredients in a blender. Blend until you get a smoothie like consistency. Serve chilled.

To get the most benefits you should consume fruit and vegetable smoothies immediately. If you want to make the smoothie for later consumption, drink it the same day. Store in the fridge.

Berry Yogurt

INGREDIENTS:

1 cup **Blueberries**, fresh or frozen

1 cup **Raspberries**, fresh or frozen

1 cup **Strawberries**, fresh or frozen

1 cup **Cashew nuts**, soaked *or 1 cup Plain yogurt*

1 cup **Coconut water**

EQUIPMENT:

High-speed blender, small mixing bowl, Serving glasses, measuring cups.

PREPARATION:

Step 1: Soak cashew nuts for 1-3 hours or overnight in a small mixing bowl. *(You can use plain yogurt instead of cashew nuts.)* Soaked cashews give your smoothie a milky taste without adding any milk products.

Step 2: Put all ingredients in a blender. Blend until you get a smoothie like consistency. Serve chilled.

To get the most benefits you should consume fruit and vegetable smoothies immediately. If you want to make the smoothie for later consumption, drink it the same day. Store in the fridge.

Berry Mighty

INGREDIENTS:

3 cups **Blueberries**, fresh or frozen

1 cup **Raspberries**, fresh or frozen

1 cup **Strawberries**, fresh or frozen

1 cup **Cashew nuts**, soaked *or 1 cup Plain yogurt*

1 cup **Coconut water**

EQUIPMENT:

High-speed blender, small mixing bowl, Serving glasses, measuring cups.

PREPARATION:

Step 1: Soak cashew nuts for 1-3 hours or overnight in a small mixing bowl. *(You can use plain yogurt instead of cashew nuts.)* Soaked cashews give your smoothie a milky taste without adding any milk products.

Step 2: Put all ingredients in a blender. Blend until you get a smoothie like consistency. Serve chilled.

To get the most benefits you should consume fruit and vegetable smoothies immediately. If you want to make the smoothie for later consumption, drink it the same day. Store in the fridge.

Power is in You

INGREDIENTS:

2 cups **Blueberries**, fresh or frozen

1 cup **Oats**, rolled

¼ cup **Wheatgrass**, powder

1 cup **Chia flour**

6 **Dates**, pitted

1 ½ cup **Coconut water**

EQUIPMENT:

High-speed blender, Serving glasses, measuring cups.

PREPARATION:

Put all ingredients in a blender. Blend until you get a smoothie like consistency. Serve chilled.

To get the most benefits you should consume fruit and vegetable smoothies immediately. If you want to make the smoothie for later consumption, drink it the same day. Store in the fridge.

Orange Date

INGREDIENTS:

2 **Mangos**, peeled, pitted

1 cup **Raisins**, golden

1 **Orange**, juice of

6 **Dates**, pitted

1 ½ cup **Coconut water**

EQUIPMENT:

High-speed blender, Serving glasses, measuring cups.

PREPARATION:

Put all ingredients in a blender. Blend until you get a smoothie like consistency. Serve chilled.

To get the most benefits you should consume fruit and vegetable smoothies immediately. If you want to make the smoothie for later consumption, drink it the same day. Store in the fridge.

Monday Love

INGREDIENTS:

6 **Carrots**, large, juice of

1 **Orange**, juice of

1 **Grapefruit**, juice of

2 cups **Oats**, rolled

½ cups **Strawberry powder** *(optional)*

EQUIPMENT:

High-speed blender, Serving glasses, measuring cups.

PREPARATION:

Put all ingredients in a blender. Blend until you get a smoothie like consistency. Serve chilled.

To get the most benefits you should consume fruit and vegetable smoothies immediately. If you want to make the smoothie for later consumption, drink it the same day. Store in the fridge.

Morning Blues

INGREDIENTS:

3 cups **Blueberries**, fresh or frozen

1 cup **Blackberries**, fresh or frozen

2 cups **Oats**, rolled

½ cups **Strawberry powder**

1 cup **Cashew nuts**, soaked *or 1 cup Plain yogurt*

6 **Dates**, pitted

½ cup **Coconut water**

EQUIPMENT:

High-speed blender, small mixing bowl, Serving glasses, measuring cups.

PREPARATION:

Step 1: Soak cashew nuts for 1-3 hours or overnight in a small mixing bowl. *(You can use plain yogurt instead of cashew nuts.)* Soaked cashews give your smoothie a milky taste without adding any milk products.

Step 2: Put all ingredients in a blender. Blend until you get a smoothie like consistency. Serve chilled.

To get the most benefits you should consume fruit and vegetable smoothies immediately. If you want to make the

smoothie for later consumption, drink it the same day. Store in the fridge.

Red

INGREDIENTS:

2 **Pomegranates**, juice of

1 cup **Raspberries**, fresh or frozen

¼ cup **Pomegranate**, powdered *(optional)*

1 cup **Cashew nuts**, soaked *or 1 cup Plain yogurt*

6 **Dates**, pitted

½ cup **Coconut water**

EQUIPMENT:

High-speed blender, small mixing bowl, Serving glasses, measuring cups.

PREPARATION:

Step 1: Soak cashew nuts for 1-3 hours or overnight in a small mixing bowl. *(You can use plain yogurt instead of cashew nuts.)* Soaked cashews give your smoothie a milky taste without adding any milk products.

Step 2: Put all ingredients in a blender. Blend until you get a smoothie like consistency. Serve chilled.

To get the most benefits you should consume fruit and vegetable smoothies immediately. If you want to make the smoothie for later consumption, drink it the same day. Store

in the fridge.

Morning Detox

INGREDIENTS:

1 **Grapefruit**, juice of

3 cups **Kale**, fresh

2 cups **Spinach**, fresh

½ **Lime**, peeled

EQUIPMENT:

High-speed blender, Serving glasses, measuring cups.

PREPARATION:

Put all ingredients in a blender. Blend until you get a smoothie like consistency. Serve chilled.

To get the most benefits you should consume fruit and vegetable smoothies immediately. If you want to make the smoothie for later consumption, drink it the same day. Store in the fridge.

Ice-Cream for Breakfast

INGREDIENTS:

3 **Bananas**, frozen, peeled

3 cups **Blueberries**, frozen

15 **Strawberries**, frozen

1 cup **Cashew nuts**, soaked *or 1 cup Plain yogurt*

6 **Dates**, pitted

½ cup **Coconut water**

EQUIPMENT:

High-speed blender, small mixing bowl, Serving glasses, measuring cups.

PREPARATION:

Step 1: Soak cashew nuts for 1-3 hours or overnight in a small mixing bowl. *(You can use plain yogurt instead of cashew nuts.)* Soaked cashews give your smoothie a milky taste without adding any milk products.

Step 2: Put all ingredients in a blender. Blend until you get a smoothie like consistency. Serve chilled.

To get the most benefits you should consume fruit and vegetable smoothies immediately. If you want to make the smoothie for later consumption, drink it the same day. Store

in the fridge.

Red Velvet Princess Cake

INGREDIENTS:

3 Bananas, frozen, peeled

3 cups Raspberries, frozen

15 Strawberries, frozen

1 cup **Cashew nuts**, soaked *or 1 cup Plain yogurt*

10 **Dates**, pitted

½ cup **Coconut water**

EQUIPMENT:

High-speed blender, small mixing bowl, Serving glasses, measuring cups.

PREPARATION:

Step 1: Soak cashew nuts for 1-3 hours or overnight in a small mixing bowl. *(You can use plain yogurt instead of cashew nuts.)* Soaked cashews give your smoothie a milky taste without adding any milk products.

Step 2: Put all ingredients in a blender. Blend until you get a smoothie like consistency. Serve chilled.

To get the most benefits you should consume fruit and vegetable smoothies immediately. If you want to make the smoothie for later consumption, drink it the same day. Store

in the fridge.

Chocolate Princess Cake

INGREDIENTS:

3 **Bananas**, frozen, peeled

3 cups **Raspberries**, frozen

15 **Strawberries**, frozen

1 cup **Cashew nuts**, soaked *or 1 cup Plain yogurt*

10 **Dates**, pitted

4 teaspoons **Cocoa powder**, raw, unsweetened

½ cup **Coconut water**

EQUIPMENT:

High-speed blender, small mixing bowl, Serving glasses, measuring cups.

PREPARATION:

Step 1: Soak cashew nuts for 1-3 hours or overnight in a small mixing bowl. *(You can use plain yogurt instead of cashew nuts.)* Soaked cashews give your smoothie a milky taste without adding any milk products.

Step 2: Put all ingredients in a blender. Blend until you get a smoothie like consistency. Serve chilled.

To get the most benefits you should consume fruit and vegetable smoothies immediately. If you want to make the

smoothie for later consumption, drink it the same day. Store in the fridge.

Chocolate Power

INGREDIENTS:

3 **Bananas**, frozen, peeled

20 **Strawberries**, frozen

1 cup **Chia seeds**, white

10 **Dates**, pitted

4 teaspoons **Cocoa powder**, raw

½ cup **Coconut water**

EQUIPMENT:

High-speed blender, Serving glasses, measuring cups.

PREPARATION:

Put all ingredients in a blender. Blend until you get a smoothie like consistency. Serve chilled.

To get the most benefits you should consume fruit and vegetable smoothies immediately. If you want to make the smoothie for later consumption, drink it the same day. Store in the fridge.

Banana Smoothie

INGREDIENTS:

FOR THE SMOOTHIE:

2 **Bananas**, peeled

1 cup **Oats**, rolled

1 cup **Almond milk**

1 cup **Cashew nuts**, soaked *or 1 cup Plain yogurt*

2 teaspoon **Honey**, raw

2 teaspoon **Vanilla**, pure, extract

1/4 teaspoon **Cinnamon**, powder

FOR THE ALMOND MILK: *(optional)*

1 cup **Almonds,** raw

2 cups **Coconut water**

EQUIPMENT:

High-speed blender, small mixing bowl, Serving glasses, measuring cups.

PREPARATION:

MAKE THE ALMOND MILK: *(optional)*

You can prepare almond milk at home, or you can also

purchase ready to use almond milk in a store.

Put one cup of almonds and two cups of coconut water into a blender. Blend it until it reaches milky consistency. Your almond milk is ready.

MAKE THE SMOOTHIE:

Step 1: Soak cashew nuts for 1-3 hours or overnight in a small mixing bowl. *(You can use plain yogurt instead of cashew nuts.)* Soaked cashews give your smoothie a milky taste without adding any milk products.

Step 2: Put all ingredients in a blender. Blend until you get a smoothie like consistency. Serve chilled.

To get the most benefits you should consume fruit and vegetable smoothies immediately. If you want to make the smoothie for later consumption, drink it the same day. Store in the fridge.

Cake for Breakfast

INGREDIENTS:

3 **Bananas**, peeled

1 cup **Raspberries**, frozen

½ cup **Almonds**, raw

½ cup **Cashew nuts**, soaked *or ½ cup Plain yogurt*

6 **Dates**, pitted

4 teaspoons **Cocoa powder**, raw, unprocessed

½ cup **Coconut water**

EQUIPMENT:

High-speed blender, small mixing bowl, Serving glasses, measuring cups.

PREPARATION:

Step 1: Soak cashew nuts for 1-3 hours or overnight in a small mixing bowl. *(You can use plain yogurt instead of cashew nuts.)* Soaked cashews give your smoothie a milky taste without adding any milk products.

Step 2: Put all ingredients in a blender. Blend until you get a smoothie like consistency. Serve chilled.

To get the most benefits you should consume fruit and vegetable smoothies immediately. If you want to make the

smoothie for later consumption, drink it the same day. Store in the fridge.

Fresh Start

INGREDIENTS:

1 **Grapefruit**, juice of

2 **Cucumbers**, fresh

1 cup **Mint**, fresh

½ **Lime**, peeled

EQUIPMENT:

High-speed blender, Serving glasses, measuring cups.

PREPARATION:

Put all ingredients in a blender. Blend until you get a smoothie like consistency. Serve chilled.

To get the most benefits you should consume fruit and vegetable smoothies immediately. If you want to make the smoothie for later consumption, drink it the same day. Store in the fridge.

Morning Power

INGREDIENTS:

FOR THE SMOOTHIE:

3 **Bananas**, peeled

1 **Mango**, peeled, pitted

1 cup Oats, rolled

1 cup **Apricots**, dried

1 cup **Raisins**, golden, dried

½ cup **Cashew nuts**, soaked *or ½ cup Plain yogurt*

1 cup **Brazil nuts**

6 **Dates**, pitted

2 cups **Almond Milk**

½ cup **Camu-camu**, powder

FOR THE ALMOND MILK: *(optional)*

1 cup **Almonds,** raw

2 cups **Coconut water**

EQUIPMENT:

High-speed blender, small mixing bowl, Serving glasses, measuring cups.

PREPARATION:

MAKE THE ALMOND MILK: *(optional)*

You can prepare almond milk at home, or you can also purchase ready to use almond milk in a store.

Put one cup of almonds and two cups of coconut water into a blender. Blend it until it reaches milky consistency. Your almond milk is ready.

MAKE THE SMOOTHIE:

Step 1: Soak cashew nuts for 1-3 hours or overnight in a small mixing bowl. *(You can use plain yogurt instead of cashew nuts.)* Soaked cashews give your smoothie a milky taste without adding any milk products.

Step 2: Put all ingredients in a blender. Blend until you get a smoothie like consistency. Serve chilled.

To get the most benefits you should consume fruit and vegetable smoothies immediately. If you want to make the smoothie for later consumption, drink it the same day. Store in the fridge.

Bloody Mary

INGREDIENTS:

3 **Tomatoes**, fresh

1 cup **Carrot juice**

1 **Cucumber**, fresh

1 **Celery stalk**, fresh

1 cup **Cilantro**, fresh

EQUIPMENT:

High-speed blender, Serving glasses, measuring cups.

PREPARATION:

Put all ingredients in a blender. Blend until you get a smoothie like consistency. Serve chilled.

To get the most benefits you should consume fruit and vegetable smoothies immediately. If you want to make the smoothie for later consumption, drink it the same day. Store in the fridge.

Simply Tomato

INGREDIENTS:

5 **Tomatoes**, fresh

1 cup **Basil,** fresh

½ **Lime**, peeled

EQUIPMENT:

High-speed blender, Serving glasses, measuring cups.

PREPARATION:

Put all ingredients in a blender. Blend until you get a smoothie like consistency. Serve chilled.

To get the most benefits you should consume fruit and vegetable smoothies immediately. If you want to make the smoothie for later consumption, drink it the same day. Store in the fridge.

Pineapple Coconut Yogurt

INGREDIENTS:

½ **Pineapple**, fresh, peeled

2 cups **Young coconut,** the meat of

1 cup **Cashew nuts**, soaked *or 1 cup Plain yogurt*

1 cup **Brazil nuts**

6 **Dates**, pitted

2 cups **Coconut water**

EQUIPMENT:

High-speed blender, small mixing bowl, Serving glasses, measuring cups.

PREPARATION:

Step 1: Soak cashew nuts for 1-3 hours or overnight in a small mixing bowl. *(You can use plain yogurt instead of cashew nuts.)* Soaked cashews give your smoothie a milky taste without adding any milk products.

Step 2: Put all ingredients in a blender. Blend until you get a smoothie like consistency. Serve chilled.

To get the most benefits you should consume fruit and vegetable smoothies immediately. If you want to make the smoothie for later consumption, drink it the same day. Store

in the fridge.

Oats and Yogurt

INGREDIENTS:

20 **Strawberries**, fresh

1 **Banana**, peeled

2 cups **Oats**, rolled

1 cup **Cashew nuts**, soaked *or 1 cup Plain yogurt*

6 **Dates**, pitted

2 cups **Coconut water**

EQUIPMENT:

High-speed blender, small mixing bowl, Serving glasses, measuring cups.

PREPARATION:

Step 1: Soak cashew nuts for 1-3 hours or overnight in a small mixing bowl. *(You can use plain yogurt instead of cashew nuts.)* Soaked cashews give your smoothie a milky taste without adding any milk products.

Step 2: Put all ingredients in a blender. Blend until you get a smoothie like consistency. Serve chilled.

To get the most benefits you should consume fruit and vegetable smoothies immediately. If you want to make the smoothie for later consumption, drink it the same day. Store

in the fridge.

Beets Bits

INGREDIENTS:

1 **Banana**, peeled

4 teaspoons **Cocoa powder**, raw, unprocessed

½ cup **Coconut water**

1 teaspoon **Beets,** powder

EQUIPMENT:

High-speed blender, Serving glasses, measuring cups.

PREPARATION:

Put all ingredients in a blender. Blend until you get a smoothie like consistency. Serve chilled.

To get the most benefits you should consume fruit and vegetable smoothies immediately. If you want to make the smoothie for later consumption, drink it the same day. Store in the fridge.

Pineapple Blast

INGREDIENTS:

½ **Pineapple**, fresh, peeled

1 cup **Mint**, fresh

EQUIPMENT:

High-speed blender, Serving glasses, measuring cups.

PREPARATION:

Put all ingredients in a blender. Blend until you get a smoothie like consistency. Serve chilled.

To get the most benefits you should consume fruit and vegetable smoothies immediately. If you want to make the smoothie for later consumption, drink it the same day. Store in the fridge.

Mango-Mango

INGREDIENTS:

3 **Mangos**, peeled, pitted

1 cup **Cashew nuts**, soaked *or 1 cup Plain yogurt*

6 **Dates**, pitted

1 cup **Coconut water**

EQUIPMENT:

High-speed blender, small mixing bowl, Serving glasses, measuring cups.

PREPARATION:

Step 1: Soak cashew nuts for 1-3 hours or overnight in a small mixing bowl. *(You can use plain yogurt instead of cashew nuts.)* Soaked cashews give your smoothie a milky taste without adding any milk products.

Step 2: Put all ingredients in a blender. Blend until you get a smoothie like consistency. Serve chilled.

To get the most benefits you should consume fruit and vegetable smoothies immediately. If you want to make the smoothie for later consumption, drink it the same day. Store in the fridge.

Morning Cleanse

INGREDIENTS:

5 cups **Orange juice,** freshly squeezed

1 **Lime**, peeled

½ inch **Ginger**, root

EQUIPMENT:

High-speed blender, Serving glasses, measuring cups.

PREPARATION:

Put all ingredients in a blender. Blend until you get a smoothie like consistency. Serve chilled.

To get the most benefits you should consume fruit and vegetable smoothies immediately. If you want to make the smoothie for later consumption, drink it the same day. Store in the fridge.

Power Run

INGREDIENTS:

FOR THE SMOOTHIE:

½ cup **Kelp,** powder, organic

2 **Bananas**, peeled

4 **Dates**, pitted

2 cups **Almond milk**

½ cup **Carob**, powder

2 teaspoons **Honey**, raw

FOR THE ALMOND MILK: *(optional)*

1 cup **Almonds,** raw

2 cups **Coconut water**

EQUIPMENT:

High-speed blender, small mixing bowl, Serving glasses, measuring cups.

PREPARATION:

MAKE THE ALMOND MILK: *(optional)*

You can prepare almond milk at home, or you can also purchase ready to use almond milk in a store.

Put one cup of almonds and two cups of coconut water into a blender. Blend it until it reaches milky consistency. Your almond milk is ready.

MAKE THE SMOOTHIE:

Step 1: Soak cashew nuts for 1-3 hours or overnight in a small mixing bowl. *(You can use plain yogurt instead of cashew nuts.)* Soaked cashews give your smoothie a milky taste without adding any milk products.

Step 2: Put all ingredients in a blender. Blend until you get a smoothie like consistency. Serve chilled.

To get the most benefits you should consume fruit and vegetable smoothies immediately. If you want to make the smoothie for later consumption, drink it the same day. Store in the fridge.

Faster than a Bullet

INGREDIENTS:

FOR THE SMOOTHIE:

¼ cup **Camu-Camu**, powder

1 **Avocado**, peeled, pitted

1 **Banana**, peeled

1 cup **Blueberries**, fresh or frozen

3 cups **Almond milk**

1 cup **Oats**, rolled

1 cup **Raisins**, golden

2 teaspoons **Honey**, raw

FOR THE ALMOND MILK: *(optional)*

1 cup **Almonds,** raw

2 cups **Coconut water**

EQUIPMENT:

High-speed blender, small mixing bowl, Serving glasses, measuring cups.

PREPARATION:

MAKE THE ALMOND MILK: *(optional)*

You can prepare almond milk at home, or you can also purchase ready to use almond milk in a store.

Put one cup of almonds and two cups of coconut water into a blender. Blend it until it reaches milky consistency. Your almond milk is ready.

MAKE THE SMOOTHIE:

Step 1: Soak cashew nuts for 1-3 hours or overnight in a small mixing bowl. *(You can use plain yogurt instead of cashew nuts.)* Soaked cashews give your smoothie a milky taste without adding any milk products.

Step 2: Put all ingredients in a blender. Blend until you get a smoothie like consistency. Serve chilled.

To get the most benefits you should consume fruit and vegetable smoothies immediately. If you want to make the smoothie for later consumption, drink it the same day. Store in the fridge.

2 Fast 4 You

INGREDIENTS:

FOR THE SMOOTHIE:

¼ cup **Chia flour**

1 **Avocado**, peeled, pitted

¼ cup **Wheatgrass,** powder

1 cup **Blueberries**, fresh or frozen

6 **Strawberries**, fresh or frozen

2 cups **Almond milk**

6 **Dates**, raw, pitted

FOR THE ALMOND MILK: *(optional)*

1 cup **Almonds,** raw

2 cups **Coconut water**

EQUIPMENT:

High-speed blender, small mixing bowl, Serving glasses, measuring cups.

PREPARATION:

MAKE THE ALMOND MILK: *(optional)*

You can prepare almond milk at home, or you can also

purchase ready to use almond milk in a store.

Put one cup of almonds and two cups of coconut water into a blender. Blend it until it reaches milky consistency. Your almond milk is ready.

MAKE THE SMOOTHIE:

Step 1: Soak cashew nuts for 1-3 hours or overnight in a small mixing bowl. *(You can use plain yogurt instead of cashew nuts.)* Soaked cashews give your smoothie a milky taste without adding any milk products.

Step 2: Put all ingredients in a blender. Blend until you get a smoothie like consistency. Serve chilled.

To get the most benefits you should consume fruit and vegetable smoothies immediately. If you want to make the smoothie for later consumption, drink it the same day. Store in the fridge.

Power Morning

INGREDIENTS:

FOR THE SMOOTHIE:

¼ cup **Alfalfa**, powder, organic

1 **Avocado**, peeled, pitted

½ cup **Wheatgrass**, powder

2 **Bananas**, peeled

1 **Mango**, peeled, pitted

2 cups **Almond milk**

1 cup **Oats**, rolled

6 **Figs**, dried

FOR THE ALMOND MILK: *(optional)*

1 cup **Almonds,** raw

2 cups **Coconut water**

EQUIPMENT:

High-speed blender, small mixing bowl, Serving glasses, measuring cups.

PREPARATION:

MAKE THE ALMOND MILK: *(optional)*

You can prepare almond milk at home, or you can also purchase ready to use almond milk in a store.

Put one cup of almonds and two cups of coconut water into a blender. Blend it until it reaches milky consistency. Your almond milk is ready.

MAKE THE SMOOTHIE:

Step 1: Soak cashew nuts for 1-3 hours or overnight in a small mixing bowl. *(You can use plain yogurt instead of cashew nuts.)* Soaked cashews give your smoothie a milky taste without adding any milk products.

Step 2: Put all ingredients in a blender. Blend until you get a smoothie like consistency. Serve chilled.

To get the most benefits you should consume fruit and vegetable smoothies immediately. If you want to make the smoothie for later consumption, drink it the same day. Store in the fridge.

Super Powers

INGREDIENTS:

FOR THE SMOOTHIE:

2 cups **Kale**, fresh, raw

2 **Bananas**, peeled

1 **Avocado**, peeled, pitted

¼ cup **Wheatgrass**, powder

2 cups **Almond milk**

FOR THE ALMOND MILK: *(optional)*

1 cup **Almonds,** raw

2 cups **Coconut water**

EQUIPMENT:

High-speed blender, small mixing bowl, Serving glasses, measuring cups.

PREPARATION:

MAKE THE ALMOND MILK: *(optional)*

You can prepare almond milk at home, or you can also purchase ready to use almond milk in a store.

Put one cup of almonds and two cups of coconut water into a blender. Blend it until it reaches milky consistency. Your almond milk is ready.

MAKE THE SMOOTHIE:

Step 1: Soak cashew nuts for 1-3 hours or overnight in a small mixing bowl. *(You can use plain yogurt instead of cashew nuts.)* Soaked cashews give your smoothie a milky taste without adding any milk products.

Step 2: Put all ingredients in a blender. Blend until you get a smoothie like consistency. Serve chilled.

To get the most benefits you should consume fruit and vegetable smoothies immediately. If you want to make the smoothie for later consumption, drink it the same day. Store in the fridge.

Green Power

INGREDIENTS:

FOR THE SMOOTHIE:

2 cups **Spinach**, fresh, raw

1 **Avocado**, peeled, pitted

1 cup **Blueberries**, fresh or frozen

¼ cup **Wheatgrass,** powder

2 cups **Almond milk**

FOR THE ALMOND MILK: *(optional)*

1 cup **Almonds,** raw

2 cups **Coconut water**

EQUIPMENT:

High-speed blender, small mixing bowl, Serving glasses, measuring cups.

PREPARATION:

MAKE THE ALMOND MILK: *(optional)*

You can prepare almond milk at home, or you can also purchase ready to use almond milk in a store.

Put one cup of almonds and two cups of coconut water into a blender. Blend it until it reaches milky consistency. Your almond milk is ready.

MAKE THE SMOOTHIE:

Step 1: Soak cashew nuts for 1-3 hours or overnight in a small mixing bowl. *(You can use plain yogurt instead of cashew nuts.)* Soaked cashews give your smoothie a milky taste without adding any milk products.

Step 2: Put all ingredients in a blender. Blend until you get a smoothie like consistency. Serve chilled.

To get the most benefits you should consume fruit and vegetable smoothies immediately. If you want to make the smoothie for later consumption, drink it the same day. Store in the fridge.

Berries All-Mighty

INGREDIENTS:

1 cup **Raspberries**, fresh or frozen

1 cup **Blueberries**, fresh or frozen

10 **Strawberries**, fresh or frozen

2 cups **Tea**, green

EQUIPMENT:

High-speed blender, Serving glasses, measuring cups.

PREPARATION:

Put all ingredients in a blender. Blend until you get a smoothie like consistency. Serve chilled.

To get the most benefits you should consume fruit and vegetable smoothies immediately. If you want to make the smoothie for later consumption, drink it the same day. Store in the fridge.

I Can Do It

INGREDIENTS:

¼ cup **Strawberry powder**, organic (*or ¼ cup of fresh strawberries*)

¼ cup **Wheatgrass,** powder

3 tablespoons **Spirulina,** powder

2 cups **Blueberries,** fresh or frozen

2 cups **Tea,** green

EQUIPMENT:

High-speed blender, Serving glasses, measuring cups.

PREPARATION:

Put all ingredients in a blender. Blend until you get a smoothie like consistency. Serve chilled.

To get the most benefits you should consume fruit and vegetable smoothies immediately. If you want to make the smoothie for later consumption, drink it the same day. Store in the fridge.

Love is Power

INGREDIENTS:

10 **Strawberries**, fresh or frozen

¼ cup **Wheatgrass,** powder

1 cup **Oats,** rolled

¼ cup **White chia**, powder

1 **Banana,** peeled

1 cup **Tea**, green

EQUIPMENT:

High-speed blender, Serving glasses, measuring cups.

PREPARATION:

Put all ingredients in a blender. Blend until you get a smoothie like consistency. Serve chilled.

To get the most benefits you should consume fruit and vegetable smoothies immediately. If you want to make the smoothie for later consumption, drink it the same day. Store in the fridge.

Turbo Charged

INGREDIENTS:

2 cups **Blueberries**, fresh or frozen

1 cup **Spinach**, fresh

3 teaspoons **Wheatgrass**, powder

1/2 cup **Oats,** rolled

1 **Avocado,** peeled, pitted

1 cup **Young coconut,** the meat of

1 cup **Coconut water**

EQUIPMENT:

High-speed blender, Serving glasses, measuring cups.

PREPARATION:

Put all ingredients in a blender. Blend until you get a smoothie like consistency. Serve chilled.

To get the most benefits you should consume fruit and vegetable smoothies immediately. If you want to make the smoothie for later consumption, drink it the same day. Store in the fridge.

Neon Green Mustang

INGREDIENTS:

2 **Kiwis**, peeled

1 cup **Spinach**, fresh

4 teaspoons **Wheatgrass,** powder

1 **Orange,** juice of

EQUIPMENT:

High-speed blender, Serving glasses, measuring cups.

PREPARATION:

Put all ingredients in a blender. Blend until you get a smoothie like consistency. Serve chilled.

To get the most benefits you should consume fruit and vegetable smoothies immediately. If you want to make the smoothie for later consumption, drink it the same day. Store in the fridge.

Red Barbie Mobile

INGREDIENTS:

10 **Strawberries**, fresh

1 cup **Spinach**, fresh

2 teaspoons **Maca,** powder *(optional)*

1 **Pomegranate,** juice of

EQUIPMENT:

High-speed blender, Serving glasses, measuring cups.

PREPARATION:

Put all ingredients in a blender. Blend until you get a smoothie like consistency. Serve chilled.

To get the most benefits you should consume fruit and vegetable smoothies immediately. If you want to make the smoothie for later consumption, drink it the same day. Store in the fridge.

Wild Mustang

INGREDIENTS:

1 cup **Blueberries,** fresh or frozen

1 **Banana,** peeled

1 cup **Spinach,** fresh

½ cup **Chia flour**

½ cup **Oats,** rolled

1 **Pomegranate,** juice of

EQUIPMENT:

High-speed blender, Serving glasses, measuring cups.

PREPARATION:

Put all ingredients in a blender. Blend until you get a smoothie like consistency. Serve chilled.

To get the most benefits you should consume fruit and vegetable smoothies immediately. If you want to make the smoothie for later consumption, drink it the same day. Store in the fridge.

All-Mighty Berries

INGREDIENTS:

1 cup **Blueberries**, fresh or frozen

1 cup **Raspberries**, fresh or frozen

10 **Strawberries,** fresh or frozen

½ cup **Oats,** rolled

1 **Pomegranate,** juice of

EQUIPMENT:

High-speed blender, Serving glasses, measuring cups.

PREPARATION:

Put all ingredients in a blender. Blend until you get a smoothie like consistency. Serve chilled.

To get the most benefits you should consume fruit and vegetable smoothies immediately. If you want to make the smoothie for later consumption, drink it the same day. Store in the fridge.

An Apple a Day...

INGREDIENTS:

1 **Apple,** peeled, pitted

1 cup **Raspberries,** fresh or frozen

10 **Strawberries,** fresh or frozen

½ cup **Oats,** rolled

1 **Orange,** juice of

EQUIPMENT:

High-speed blender, Serving glasses, measuring cups.

PREPARATION:

Put all ingredients in a blender. Blend until you get a smoothie like consistency. Serve chilled.

To get the most benefits you should consume fruit and vegetable smoothies immediately. If you want to make the smoothie for later consumption, drink it the same day. Store in the fridge.

Nuts and Bolts

INGREDIENTS:

FOR THE SMOOTHIE:

2 **Bananas**, peeled

1 cup **Raisins,** golden

½ cup **Oats,** rolled

1 cup **Almond milk**

1 cup **Cashew nuts**, soaked *or 1 cup Plain yogurt*

2 teaspoons **Honey,** raw

FOR THE ALMOND MILK: *(optional)*

1 cup **Almonds,** raw

2 cups **Coconut water**

EQUIPMENT:

High-speed blender, small mixing bowl, Serving glasses, measuring cups.

PREPARATION:

MAKE THE ALMOND MILK: *(optional)*

You can prepare almond milk at home, or you can also purchase ready to use almond milk in a store.

Put one cup of almonds and two cups of coconut water into a blender. Blend it until it reaches milky consistency. Your almond milk is ready.

MAKE THE SMOOTHIE:

Step 1: Soak cashew nuts for 1-3 hours or overnight in a small mixing bowl. *(You can use plain yogurt instead of cashew nuts.)* Soaked cashews give your smoothie a milky taste without adding any milk products.

Step 2: Put all ingredients in a blender. Blend until you get a smoothie like consistency. Serve chilled.

To get the most benefits you should consume fruit and vegetable smoothies immediately. If you want to make the smoothie for later consumption, drink it the same day. Store in the fridge.

Strawberry Dreams

INGREDIENTS:

FOR THE SMOOTHIE:

2 **Bananas**, peeled

10 **Strawberries**, fresh or frozen

1 cup **Oats**, rolled

1 cup **Almond milk**

1 cup **Cashew nuts**, soaked *or 1 cup Plain yogurt*

4 **Dates**, pitted

FOR THE ALMOND MILK: *(optional)*

1 cup **Almonds,** raw

2 cups **Coconut water**

EQUIPMENT:

High-speed blender, small mixing bowl, Serving glasses, measuring cups.

PREPARATION:

MAKE THE ALMOND MILK: *(optional)*

You can prepare almond milk at home, or you can also purchase ready to use almond milk in a store.

Put one cup of almonds and two cups of coconut water into a blender. Blend it until it reaches milky consistency. Your almond milk is ready.

MAKE THE SMOOTHIE:

Step 1: Soak cashew nuts for 1-3 hours or overnight in a small mixing bowl. *(You can use plain yogurt instead of cashew nuts.)* Soaked cashews give your smoothie a milky taste without adding any milk products.

Step 2: Put all ingredients in a blender. Blend until you get a smoothie like consistency. Serve chilled.

To get the most benefits you should consume fruit and vegetable smoothies immediately. If you want to make the smoothie for later consumption, drink it the same day. Store in the fridge.

Banana Boat

INGREDIENTS:

FOR THE SMOOTHIE:

1 **Banana**, peeled

7 **Strawberries**, fresh or frozen

1 cup **Blueberries**, fresh or frozen

1 cup **White chia flour** (or rolled oats)

1 cup **Almond milk**

1 cup **Cashew nuts**, soaked or 1 cup Plain yogurt

4 **Dates**, pitted

FOR THE ALMOND MILK: (optional)

1 cup **Almonds,** raw

2 cups **Coconut water**

EQUIPMENT:

High-speed blender, small mixing bowl, Serving glasses, measuring cups.

PREPARATION:

MAKE THE ALMOND MILK: (optional)

You can prepare almond milk at home, or you can also

purchase ready to use almond milk in a store.

Put one cup of almonds and two cups of coconut water into a blender. Blend it until it reaches milky consistency. Your almond milk is ready.

MAKE THE SMOOTHIE:

Step 1: Soak cashew nuts for 1-3 hours or overnight in a small mixing bowl. *(You can use plain yogurt instead of cashew nuts.)* Soaked cashews give your smoothie a milky taste without adding any milk products.

Step 2: Put all ingredients in a blender. Blend until you get a smoothie like consistency. Serve chilled.

To get the most benefits you should consume fruit and vegetable smoothies immediately. If you want to make the smoothie for later consumption, drink it the same day. Store in the fridge.

Vanilla Chocolate

INGREDIENTS:

FOR THE SMOOTHIE:

2 **Bananas**, peeled

1 cup **Raspberries,** fresh or frozen

1 cup **Almond milk**

1 cup **Cashew nuts**, soaked *or 1 cup Plain yogurt*

2 teaspoons **Cocoa powder**, raw, unprocessed

1 teaspoon **Vanilla**, pure, extract

FOR THE ALMOND MILK: *(optional)*

1 cup **Almonds,** raw

2 cups **Coconut water**

EQUIPMENT:

High-speed blender, small mixing bowl, Serving glasses, measuring cups.

PREPARATION:

MAKE THE ALMOND MILK: *(optional)*

You can prepare almond milk at home, or you can also purchase ready to use almond milk in a store.

Put one cup of almonds and two cups of coconut water into a blender. Blend it until it reaches milky consistency. Your almond milk is ready.

MAKE THE SMOOTHIE:

Step 1: Soak cashew nuts for 1-3 hours or overnight in a small mixing bowl. *(You can use plain yogurt instead of cashew nuts.)* Soaked cashews give your smoothie a milky taste without adding any milk products.

Step 2: Put all ingredients in a blender. Blend until you get a smoothie like consistency. Serve chilled.

To get the most benefits you should consume fruit and vegetable smoothies immediately. If you want to make the smoothie for later consumption, drink it the same day. Store in the fridge.

Green Star

INGREDIENTS:

2 cups **Broccoli,** fresh

1 **Cucumber,** fresh

3 **Apples,** peeled, pitted

1 **Avocado,** peeled, pitted

1 cup **Brazilian nuts** *(or Cashews)*

1 **Lime**, peeled, pitted

EQUIPMENT:

High-speed blender, Serving glasses, measuring cups.

PREPARATION:

Put all ingredients in a blender. Blend until you get a smoothie like consistency. Serve chilled.

To get the most benefits you should consume fruit and vegetable smoothies immediately. If you want to make the smoothie for later consumption, drink it the same day. Store in the fridge.

Grape Go Green

INGREDIENTS:

2 cups **Spinach,** fresh

1 cup **Collard,** greens, chopped

2 cups **Grapes,** green

1 **Grapefruit,** juice of

½ **Lime,** peeled, pitted

EQUIPMENT:

High-speed blender, Serving glasses, measuring cups.

PREPARATION:

Put all ingredients in a blender. Blend until you get a smoothie like consistency. Serve chilled.

To get the most benefits you should consume fruit and vegetable smoothies immediately. If you want to make the smoothie for later consumption, drink it the same day. Store in the fridge.

Red Rainbow

INGREDIENTS:

1 cup **Raspberries,** fresh or frozen

10 **Strawberries,** fresh or frozen

1 cup **Cherries,** pitted, fresh or frozen

1 **Pomegranate,** juice of

1 cup **White chia flour**

EQUIPMENT:

High-speed blender, Serving glasses, measuring cups.

PREPARATION:

Put all ingredients in a blender. Blend until you get a smoothie like consistency. Serve chilled.

To get the most benefits you should consume fruit and vegetable smoothies immediately. If you want to make the smoothie for later consumption, drink it the same day. Store in the fridge.

Orange Rainbow

INGREDIENTS:

4 **Apricots,** raw, pitted

1 cup **Apricots,** dried, pitted

1 **Mango,** peeled, pitted

3 **Carrots,** juice of

1 **Orange,** juice of

1 cup **Chia flour,** white

EQUIPMENT:

High-speed blender, Serving glasses, measuring cups.

PREPARATION:

Put all ingredients in a blender. Blend until you get a smoothie like consistency. Serve chilled.

To get the most benefits you should consume fruit and vegetable smoothies immediately. If you want to make the smoothie for later consumption, drink it the same day. Store in the fridge.

Yellow Rainbow

INGREDIENTS:

1 **Grapefruit,** juice of

½ **Pineapple,** fresh, peeled

1 **Banana**, peeled

3 **Figs,** yellow

1 cup **Chia flour,** white

EQUIPMENT:

High-speed blender, Serving glasses, measuring cups.

PREPARATION:

Put all ingredients in a blender. Blend until you get a smoothie like consistency. Serve chilled.

To get the most benefits you should consume fruit and vegetable smoothies immediately. If you want to make the smoothie for later consumption, drink it the same day. Store in the fridge.

Green Rainbow

INGREDIENTS:

3 teaspoon **Wheatgrass,** powder

2 **Kiwis,** fresh

1 **Cucumber,** fresh

2 cups **Grapes,** green

½ cup **Mint,** fresh

1 cup **Chia flour,** white

EQUIPMENT:

High-speed blender, Serving glasses, measuring cups.

PREPARATION:

Put all ingredients in a blender. Blend until you get a smoothie like consistency. Serve chilled.

To get the most benefits you should consume fruit and vegetable smoothies immediately. If you want to make the smoothie for later consumption, drink it the same day. Store in the fridge.

Purple Rainbow

INGREDIENTS:

2 cup **Grapes,** purple

2 **Carrots,** purple

½ cup **Raisins,** golden

4 **Prunes,** dried, pitted

1 cup **Cashew nuts**, soaked *or 1 cup Plain yogurt*

1 cup **Tea**, green

EQUIPMENT:

High-speed blender, small mixing bowl, Serving glasses, measuring cups.

PREPARATION:

Step 1: Soak cashew nuts for 1-3 hours or overnight in a small mixing bowl. *(You can use plain yogurt instead of cashew nuts.)* Soaked cashews give your smoothie a milky taste without adding any milk products.

Step 2: Put all ingredients in a blender. Blend until you get a smoothie like consistency. Serve chilled.

To get the most benefits you should consume fruit and vegetable smoothies immediately. If you want to make the smoothie for later consumption, drink it the same day. Store

in the fridge.

White Rainbow

INGREDIENTS:

5 **Pears,** white

5 **Nectarines,** white

1 cup **Chia flour,** white *(or oats, rolled)*

½ inch **Ginger,** fresh

1 cup **Coconut water**

EQUIPMENT:

High-speed blender, Serving glasses, measuring cups.

PREPARATION:

Put all ingredients in a blender. Blend until you get a smoothie like consistency. Serve chilled.

To get the most benefits you should consume fruit and vegetable smoothies immediately. If you want to make the smoothie for later consumption, drink it the same day. Store in the fridge.

Strawberry Simple

INGREDIENTS:

15 **Strawberries**, fresh or frozen

½ cup **Cashews,** soaked for one hour or overnight

1 cup **Chia flour,** white *(or **oats,** rolled)*

1 cup **Young coconut,** the meat of

1 cup **Coconut water**

EQUIPMENT:

High-speed blender, Serving glasses, measuring cups.

PREPARATION:

Put all ingredients in a blender. Blend until you get a smoothie like consistency. Serve chilled.

To get the most benefits you should consume fruit and vegetable smoothies immediately. If you want to make the smoothie for later consumption, drink it the same day. Store in the fridge.

Royal Raspberry

INGREDIENTS:

3 cups **Raspberries,** fresh or frozen

1 cup **Cashews,** soaked for one hour or overnight

1 cup **Chia flour,** white *(or oats, rolled)*

1 cup **Young coconut,** the meat of

1 cup **Coconut water**

EQUIPMENT:

High-speed blender, Serving glasses, measuring cups.

PREPARATION:

Put all ingredients in a blender. Blend until you get a smoothie like consistency. Serve chilled.

To get the most benefits you should consume fruit and vegetable smoothies immediately. If you want to make the smoothie for later consumption, drink it the same day. Store in the fridge.

Banana Avocado

INGREDIENTS:

2 **Bananas,** peeled

1 **Avocado,** peeled, pitted

1 cup **Oats**, rolled

2 **Pears,** peeled, pitted

½ cup **Mint,** fresh

1 cup **Coconut water**

EQUIPMENT:

High-speed blender, Serving glasses, measuring cups.

PREPARATION:

Put all ingredients in a blender. Blend until you get a smoothie like consistency. Serve chilled.

To get the most benefits you should consume fruit and vegetable smoothies immediately. If you want to make the smoothie for later consumption, drink it the same day. Store in the fridge.

Tropical Strom

INGREDIENTS:

½ **Pineapple,** peeled

1 **Avocado,** peeled, pitted

1 **Banana**, peeled

2 cups **Young coconut,** the meat of

1 cup **Chia four,** white *(or **oats**, rolled)*

1 **Orange,** juice of

EQUIPMENT:

High-speed blender, Serving glasses, measuring cups.

PREPARATION:

Put all ingredients in a blender. Blend until you get a smoothie like consistency. Serve chilled.

To get the most benefits you should consume fruit and vegetable smoothies immediately. If you want to make the smoothie for later consumption, drink it the same day. Store in the fridge.

Pomegranate Power Boat

INGREDIENTS:

1 **Pomegranate,** juice of

1 **Avocado,** peeled, pitted

10 **Strawberries,** fresh or frozen

3 teaspoons **Maca,** powder

EQUIPMENT:

High-speed blender, Serving glasses, measuring cups.

PREPARATION:

Put all ingredients in a blender. Blend until you get a smoothie like consistency. Serve chilled.

To get the most benefits you should consume fruit and vegetable smoothies immediately. If you want to make the smoothie for later consumption, drink it the same day. Store in the fridge.

Tomato Powerhouse

INGREDIENTS:

3 **Tomatoes,** fresh

1 **Avocado,** peeled, pitted

1 cup **Cilantro,** fresh

1 teaspoon **Wheatgrass,** powder

1 **Lime,** peeled, pitted

1 cup **Tea**, green

EQUIPMENT:

High-speed blender, Serving glasses, measuring cups.

PREPARATION:

Put all ingredients in a blender. Blend until you get a smoothie like consistency. Serve chilled.

To get the most benefits you should consume fruit and vegetable smoothies immediately. If you want to make the smoothie for later consumption, drink it the same day. Store in the fridge.

Tomato Cucumber Crunch

INGREDIENTS:

3 **Tomatoes,** fresh

1 **Avocado,** peeled, pitted

3 **Celery stalks,** fresh

1 cup **Parsley,** fresh

1 **Cucumber,** fresh

1 **Red pepper,** fresh

1 **Lime,** peeled, pitted

EQUIPMENT:

High-speed blender, Serving glasses, measuring cups.

PREPARATION:

Put all ingredients in a blender. Blend until you get a smoothie like consistency. Serve chilled.

To get the most benefits you should consume fruit and vegetable smoothies immediately. If you want to make the smoothie for later consumption, drink it the same day. Store in the fridge.

Cucumber Crunch

INGREDIENTS:

1 **Cucumber,** fresh

1 **Grapefruit**, fresh

1 **Lime**, peeled, pitted

1 cup **Kale**, fresh

½ cup **Mint**, fresh

EQUIPMENT:

High-speed blender, Serving glasses, measuring cups.

PREPARATION:

Put all ingredients in a blender. Blend until you get a smoothie like consistency. Serve chilled.

To get the most benefits you should consume fruit and vegetable smoothies immediately. If you want to make the smoothie for later consumption, drink it the same day. Store in the fridge.

Power Breakfast

INGREDIENTS:

1 cup **Raisins,** brown

1 cup **Oats,** rolled

1 cup **Cranberries,** dried

1 **Banana,** peeled

½ cup **Almonds,** raw

1 cup **Young coconut,** the meat of

1 cup **Coconut water**

EQUIPMENT:

High-speed blender, Serving glasses, measuring cups.

PREPARATION:

Put all ingredients in a blender. Blend until you get a smoothie like consistency. Serve chilled.

To get the most benefits you should consume fruit and vegetable smoothies immediately. If you want to make the smoothie for later consumption, drink it the same day. Store in the fridge.

Sunny Power Breakfast

INGREDIENTS:

10 **Strawberries,** fresh or frozen

1 cup **Raisins,** golden

1 cup **Oats,** rolled

1 **Banana,** peeled

1 cup **Cashews,** soaked for one hour or overnight

1 cup **Young coconut,** the meat of

1 cup **Coconut water**

EQUIPMENT:

High-speed blender, Serving glasses, measuring cups.

PREPARATION:

Put all ingredients in a blender. Blend until you get a smoothie like consistency. Serve chilled.

To get the most benefits you should consume fruit and vegetable smoothies immediately. If you want to make the smoothie for later consumption, drink it the same day. Store in the fridge.

Green Sunshine Power

INGREDIENTS:

3 teaspoons **Wheatgrass,** powder

1 cup **Cauliflower,** florets

1 cup **Cilantro,** fresh

1 **Grapefruit,** juice of

1 **Banana,** peeled

2 teaspoons **Maca,** powder

1 cup **Chia flour,** white

1 cup **Coconut water**

EQUIPMENT:

High-speed blender, Serving glasses, measuring cups.

PREPARATION:

Put all ingredients in a blender. Blend until you get a smoothie like consistency. Serve chilled.

To get the most benefits you should consume fruit and vegetable smoothies immediately. If you want to make the smoothie for later consumption, drink it the same day. Store in the fridge.

Purple Power Madness

INGREDIENTS:

1 **Pomegranate,** juice of

5 **Prunes,** dried, pitted

1 cup **Young coconut**, the meat of

4 **Dated,** pitted

2 teaspoons **Maca,** Powder

1 cup **Chia flour,** white

1 cup **Coconut water**

EQUIPMENT:

High-speed blender, Serving glasses, measuring cups.

PREPARATION:

Put all ingredients in a blender. Blend until you get a smoothie like consistency. Serve chilled.

To get the most benefits you should consume fruit and vegetable smoothies immediately. If you want to make the smoothie for later consumption, drink it the same day. Store in the fridge.

Tomato Salad

INGREDIENTS:

2 **Tomatoes,** fresh

3 cups **Lettuce,** fresh

1 cup **Kelp,** powder

1 cup **Kale,** fresh

1 **Pepper,** red, fresh

1 **Cucumber,** fresh

½ cup **Cilantro,** fresh

1 **Lime,** peeled, pitted

EQUIPMENT:

High-speed blender, Serving glasses, measuring cups.

PREPARATION:

Put all ingredients in a blender. Blend until you get a smoothie like consistency. Serve chilled.

To get the most benefits you should consume fruit and vegetable smoothies immediately. If you want to make the smoothie for later consumption, drink it the same day. Store in the fridge.

Green Power Salad

INGREDIENTS:

1 **Cucumber,** fresh

2 **Tomatoes,** fresh

1 cup **Cranberries,** fresh or frozen

3 cups **Lettuce**, fresh

2 teaspoons Maca Powder

1 cup Spinach, fresh

1 Pepper, red, fresh

1 Lime, peeled, pitted

EQUIPMENT:

High-speed blender, Serving glasses, measuring cups.

PREPARATION:

Put all ingredients in a blender. Blend until you get a smoothie like consistency. Serve chilled.

To get the most benefits you should consume fruit and vegetable smoothies immediately. If you want to make the smoothie for later consumption, drink it the same day. Store in the fridge.

Pure Power

INGREDIENTS:

1 cup **Kelp,** powder

2 teaspoons **Wheatgrass,** power

1 **Cucumber,** fresh

1 cup **Spinach,** fresh

1 **Grapefruit,** juice of

1 **Orange,** juice of

1 **Lime,** juice of

EQUIPMENT:

High-speed blender, Serving glasses, measuring cups.

PREPARATION:

Put all ingredients in a blender. Blend until you get a smoothie like consistency. Serve chilled.

To get the most benefits you should consume fruit and vegetable smoothies immediately. If you want to make the smoothie for later consumption, drink it the same day. Store in the fridge.

Kale Orange

INGREDIENTS:

1 cup **Kale,** fresh

1 **Orange,** juice of

½ cup **Chia flour,** white

1 **Banana,** peeled

1 **Lime,** peeled, pitted

EQUIPMENT:

High-speed blender, Serving glasses, measuring cups.

PREPARATION:

Put all ingredients in a blender. Blend until you get a smoothie like consistency. Serve chilled.

To get the most benefits you should consume fruit and vegetable smoothies immediately. If you want to make the smoothie for later consumption, drink it the same day. Store in the fridge.

Spinach Spin

INGREDIENTS:

1 cup **Spinach**, fresh

1 **Cucumber**, fresh

½ **Avocado**, peeled, pitted

1 cup **Blueberries,** fresh or frozen

3 teaspoons **Kelp,** powder

1 cup **Oats,** rolled

EQUIPMENT:

High-speed blender, Serving glasses, measuring cups.

PREPARATION:

Put all ingredients in a blender. Blend until you get a smoothie like consistency. Serve chilled.

To get the most benefits you should consume fruit and vegetable smoothies immediately. If you want to make the smoothie for later consumption, drink it the same day. Store in the fridge.

MARIA SOBININA   BRILLIANTkitchenideas.com

Chia Blueberries

INGREDIENTS:

2 cups **Blueberries,** fresh or frozen

1 cup **Cranberries,** dried

1 **Banana,** peeled

½ cup **Chia flour,** white

1 cup **Coconut water**

EQUIPMENT:

High-speed blender, Serving glasses, measuring cups.

PREPARATION:

Put all ingredients in a blender. Blend until you get a smoothie like consistency. Serve chilled.

To get the most benefits you should consume fruit and vegetable smoothies immediately. If you want to make the smoothie for later consumption, drink it the same day. Store in the fridge.

Chia Strawberries

INGREDIENTS:

2 cups **Strawberries,** fresh or frozen

1 cup **Cranberries,** dried

1 **Banana,** peeled

½ cup **Chia flour,** white

1 cup **Coconut water**

EQUIPMENT:

High-speed blender, Serving glasses, measuring cups.

PREPARATION:

Put all ingredients in a blender. Blend until you get a smoothie like consistency. Serve chilled.

To get the most benefits you should consume fruit and vegetable smoothies immediately. If you want to make the smoothie for later consumption, drink it the same day. Store in the fridge.

Thank You for Purchasing This Book!

I create and test recipes for you. I hope you enjoyed these recipes.

Your review of this book helps me succeed & grow. If you enjoyed this book, please leave me a short (1-2 sentence) review on Amazon.

Thank you so much for reviewing this book!

Do you have any questions?
Email me at: **Maria@BRILLIANTkithenideas.com**

MARIA SOBININA
BRILLIANT kitchen ideas

Would you like to learn cooking techniques and tips?
Visit us at:

www. BRILLIANTkitchenideas.com